PRAISE FOR

Everything Starts from Prayer

"Mother Teresa's life was a living prayer.
with God and how all of us can reach 1
—MARIANNE W

"With the publication of *Everything Starts fro.. ..ayer*, Mother Teresa continues to bless us from beyond the grave. These kernels of truth from the nun in Calcutta provide food for the soul. Her messages, though short on words, are deep in wisdom and spiritual insight, and hold meaning for people of all faiths."

—MOST REVEREND ANTHONY M. PILLA, Bishop of Cleveland,
President, National Conference of Catholic Bishops

"Dr. Stern's editorial hand is sure and judicious; the selection of material reveals the mystical realization behind Mother Teresa's powerful encomium to prayer in an all-inclusive sense. Thus, the passages are not only spiritually inspiring (as one would, of course, expect), but intellectually compelling as well. Well done."

—LOU NORDSTROM, American Zen Teacher, White Plum lineage

"Dr. Stern deserves to be congratulated for *Everything Starts from Prayer*, an inspiring book intended to foster the spiritual life of people of all faiths or none. We hope and pray that many readers will find it an invitation to pray."

—FATHER EDWARD LE JOLY, Mother Teresa's spiritual advisor

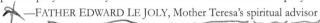

"A jewel of a book—*Everything Starts from Prayer* is a must for believers of all faiths and for seekers everywhere."

—MAURICE FRIEDMAN, author of *The Wisdom of the Heart:
Religion and Human Wholeness*

"It is wonderful that a psychiatrist whose work is to seek healing as well as understanding of human beings has thought to gather Mother Teresa's thoughts on prayer. This small book may be Mother Teresa's greatest legacy because it reveals the prayerful orientation that made her life—and can make ours—so fruitful."

—POLLY BERRIEN BERENDS, author of *Coming to Life:
Traveling the Spiritual Path in Everyday Life*

"Dr. Stern has very sensitively and carefully given us the essence of a truly spiritual person, and in the process helped make prayer in our own lives more rewarding."

—RABBI JACK BEMPORAD, Director, The Center for
Interreligious Understanding at Ramapo College

"With this simple, beautiful book, Dr. Stern has done a wonderful job making Mother Teresa's thoughts on man's relationship to God accessible to all."

—SWAMI CHETANANANDA, author of *Choose to be Happy*

"Mother Teresa is a holy mother to us all. She always has been an inspiration and reminder to me of what love can do in the world. She is the epitome of a Bodhisattva, the altruistic enlightenment-activist serving those suffering in this world."

—LAMA SURYA DAS, Tibetan Buddhist master and
author of *Awakening the Buddha Within*

"How do we start praying? Anthony Stern gives us a great gift. In this magnificent collection of Mother Teresa's words, we are shown how to cultivate our inner lives and bring forth the prayers that live within us."

—PROF. SUSANNAH HESCHEL, author of *Abraham Geiger and the Jewish Jesus*

"These beautiful prayer instructions transcend all boundaries of time and space. Here Mother Teresa is a universal figure reaching out from soul-to-soul to all those who pray or long to pray. May her words reach many and open hearts."

—RABBI ARTHUR GREEN, co-editor of *Your Word is Fire:
The Hasidic Masters on Contemplative Prayer*

"This book's contents and its title say it all. Whatever you are looking for starts with prayer. Hopefully you will read and learn that true prayer is not about personal desires, needs or religions. Mother Teresa is a role model for each of us. Pray we may became what she was, and heal the world by using prayer to lead us on the path to spirituality and God."

—BERNIE SIEGEL, M.D., author of *Love, Medicine and Miracles*

Everything
Starts
from
Prayer

SECOND
EDITION

Mother Teresa's Meditations on
Spiritual Life for People of All Faiths

Everything Starts from Prayer

SECOND
EDITION

SELECTED AND ARRANGED BY ANTHONY STERN, M.D.
WITH A FOREWORD BY LARRY DOSSEY, M.D.

White Cloud Press
Ashland, Oregon

Inquiries should be addressed to:
White Cloud Press
PO Box 3400
Ashland, Oregon 97520
www.whitecloudpress.com

10 9 8 7 6 5 4 3 2 1

First edition: October 1998
Printed in the United States of America

Cover design: Confluence Book Services
Cover and interior photos: Magnum Photos, Inc. 1997 Raghu Rai

Library of Congress Cataloging-in-Publication Data
Teresa, Mother, 1910-1997.
   Everything starts from prayer : Mother Teresa's meditations on spiritual life
for people of all faiths / selected and arranged by Anthony Stern ; foreword by
Larry Dossey.
       p. cm.
   ISBN 978-0-9745245-7-3 (pbk.) 978-0-9793840-1-1 (cloth)
   1. Prayer--Meditations. I. Stern, Anthony. II. Title.

BL560.T47 2009
204'.32--dc22
                                        2009029903

TABLE OF CONTENTS

P37 the MC's prayer to begin the day
38 " How to Be "Childlike"
41 * "SMALL RAISINGS of the MIND" - to pray / work
49 * e SONG

Foreword to the Second Edition:
Mother Teresa's Faith and Doubt

Anthony Stern, M.D.

Since the publication of this collection's first edition in 1998, letters written by Mother Teresa have revealed that she struggled with severe doubt due to a sense of inner distance from God. This has been a challenging and sobering revelation for people of faith who have idealized her. But ultimately, the revelation of Mother Teresa's inner struggle is a blessing—it undermines several pervasive myths about the spiritual journey, and it underscores a central and powerful truth about prayer.

First, Mother Teresa's doubt subverts the myth that holy people do not encounter crises and impasses. As children, we often put our elders and mentors on pedestals, but as we grow older, we come to see that the parents and leaders we admire all struggle and have a shadow side, no matter how holy, good, or beautiful they are. To discover the complexity

[handwritten margin note: M.T's DOUBT]

ix

of those we look up to is simply a part of growing up and becoming more aware adults.

Second, her struggle with inner doubt and darkness reveals the myth that the spiritual journey is a bed of roses, all sweetness and light. "Tell me, Father," Mother Teresa wrote in a letter in 1959 to Reverend Lawrence Picachy, "why is there so much pain and darkness in my soul?"[1] Like any worthy undertaking, the path to the Source of all blessings, the Divine Mystery, involves serious difficulty at times and requires tremendous perseverance. This often manifests in excruciating loneliness and inner emptiness—an arid, desolate landscape. "I am told God loves me—" she once wrote in a letter addressed to Jesus, "and yet the reality of darkness & coldness & emptiness is so great that nothing touches my soul." For some such souls, this sense of "spiritual dryness," as she called it, can stretch on for a devastatingly long period of time. As Mother Teresa's letters suggest, this was indeed true for her. By some scholars' accounts, she carried on for a half-century in total devotion to Christ while traversing an inner landscape in which she felt total abandonment by him.[2]

Third, her inner state sheds light on the myth that our own feelings are the exclusive or even the primary judge of whether our inner work is going well. It is a common mistake to base the validity of any work, spiritual or otherwise, primarily on how we feel. For example, when we love someone, we do not necessarily feel this love at all times. This has led countless teachers to say, rightly, that love is not a feeling. It includes how we feel, but it is much more than that. More than anything, love is a commitment. Mother Teresa's example of fidelity to her beloved God in the face of her perceived abandonment by him is unsurpassed. Similarly, anyone who expects to feel better because of their dedication to the inner quest is going to have trouble sustaining an effort for the long haul. It is very good to listen to one's feelings, and we all need a good outlet to express them, but to put them center-stage misses the spiritual boat.

Fourth, Mother Teresa's disquiet reveals the myth that true faith is a stranger to doubt. Anyone who has studied the lives of the saints or other holy people can likely appreciate this fact. It is through its friction with the darkness of doubt that the light of faith slowly becomes stronger, deeper, brighter. Seasoned travelers—not only beginners—on the spiritual path struggle with doubt and darkness. One religious master expressed this well when he said that to break through to spiritual realization, one needs great faith, great doubt, and great determination to reconcile the two opposing forces.

Finally, Mother Teresa's doubts about God's existence leads us to a central truth about prayer: intentional prayer only makes sense because of the very fact that we harbor the tension of doubt within us. If our bones were not sending whispers of doubt to our hearts, there would be no need for prayer at all. In a state of utterly pure faith, there is effortless silence and courage and virtue and action, without any recourse whatsoever to deliberate prayer. Most seekers eventually have a taste or two of such blessed times, or perhaps more frequent experiences of it, but no one—not even the saints—can live there all the time. The main point of prayer is that it strengthens our faith in the face of doubt, wherever we are on the sinner-saint spectrum.

In other words, doubt is inevitable. If we did not doubt, we would not be human. All human beings face pain and are prone to uncertainty, to that "terrible darkness,"[3] as Mother Teresa once described it. The question is: what do we do with this knot of pain and confusion within us? Do we get entirely lost in it, or do we accept it and oppose it and gently work to transform it through our spiritual intention and practice? We face this choice every day, just as she did. This is our spiritual training. And just as with any learning process, some days and some hours we do better than others. If we can accept this reality, we can perhaps learn more and more profoundly to be patient with ourselves. For many of us—from the spiritual leader to the nascent seeker—reaching higher ground involves that familiar dance of two steps forward, one step back. We continue progressing toward something closer to perfection while accepting our imperfections. A fitting illustration of this journey, prayer itself embodies a healthy combination of sincere aspiration tempered by honest acceptance.

In this sense, all of our prayers, even those of gratitude and thanksgiving, can be seen as echoes of the father of the epileptic son in the Gospel of Mark, who cried out from his heart to Jesus, "I believe, please help my unbelief!" In other words, "I have faith, please help my doubt!" This is an honest human prayer. Perhaps it is *the* honest human prayer, expressed in many ways. Prayer is an embodiment of the faith and the doubt alive within all of us.

Mother Teresa's doubt makes her more alive today than ever. Her honest human prayer serves as a beacon for people of all faiths, in all walks of life, who traverse that lonely and arid landscape. "If I ever become a Saint," she wrote in 1962, "I will surely be one of 'darkness.' I will continually be absent from Heaven—to [light] the light of those in darkness on earth."[4] As we imagine her lighting the light in her faithful vigil over us, let us also pray for her and all the saints, for all of our teachers and mentors, and "let us pray for each other, for this is the best way to love one another."[5] The title of this work is taken from Mother Teresa's own words: "Everything starts from prayer." Although prayer was, at times, difficult for her, I believe it was a cornerstone of her astounding faith in the face of persistent doubt. In our own prayers, may we all proceed together in a deepening bond of mutual love and support, helping each other with the pain and the doubt that is our common lot, and may we continue to grow in compassion for each other.

ENDNOTES

1. David Van Biema, "Mother Teresa's Crisis of Faith," *Time*, August 23, 2007, http://www.time.com/time/world/article /0,8599,1655415-2,00.html

2. Ibid.

3. "Letters reveal Mother Teresa's doubt about faith," Reuters India, August 25, 2007, http://in.reuters.com/article/topNews/ idINIndia-29140020070824?pageNumber=3&virtualBrandCh annel=0

4. David Van Biema, "Mother Teresa's Crisis of Faith," *Time*, August 23, 2007, http://www.time.com/time/world/article /0,8599,1655415-2,00.html

5. *Everything Starts from Prayer*, page 88.

Foreword:

Larry Dossey, M.D.

[handwritten: PRAYER IS a Bridge to the ABSOLUTE]

PRAYER IS ONE OF THE MOST ESSENTIAL ACTIVITIES OF human life. Throughout history it has nurtured our grandest visions and provided meaning and purpose to our activities. It is impossible to imagine the evolution of any culture without prayer. Prayer is universal; we know of no society where it does not take place.

Prayer has many faces. There are prayers of petition, intercession, thanksgiving, and adoration. But one thread connects all prayer: Whatever form it may take, *prayer is a bridge to the Absolute,* a way of connecting with something higher, wiser, and more powerful than the individual self.

Many people believe that prayer is too old-fashioned in our modern, scientific age, that prayer and science are incompatible, and that prayer belongs to the category of superstition and fantasy. One of the great ironies of the modern age, however, is that proponents of prayer and proponents of science are engaged in a new and amazing dialogue. This is happening in three different ways.

First, a high proportion of current scientists today believe in a Supreme Being who answers prayer. This may come as a shock to people who have been taught that genuine scientists cannot simultaneously believe in the Absolute and do good science. In 1997, however, researchers surveyed American biologists, physicists, and mathematicians about their religious beliefs.[1] They found that 39% believe in God—specifically, they believe in the kind of God who responds to prayer. The highest percentage of believers was found among mathematicians, who practice what many consider the purest kind of science that exists. And so we see that the prevalent views that science is godless, that atheists make the best scientists, and that prayer and science cannot coexist are simply stereotypes to be challenged.

Second, medical scientists studying the effects of prayer have found compelling evidence of the benefits of prayer, meditation, and relaxation on individuals who pray.[2] The body appears to *like* prayer and responds in healthy ways in the cardiovascular, immune, and other systems. But even more interesting are studies showing that intercessory or *distant* prayer also has an effect, even when the individual being prayed for is unaware of the prayer being offered and is at a great distance from the person praying. These studies are numerous, have been replicated by many scientists, and have involved not only humans but nonhumans as the prayer recipients. This latter point is important: If prayer's effects extend to animals and plants, they cannot be ascribed only to positive thinking or the placebo response.

The third major development heralding a synthesis of science and prayer is the recent emergence of scientific theories on the nature of consciousness.[3] In general, these views go beyond the old idea that the effects of the mind are confined to one's individual brain and body. These new theories permit consciousness to act outside the physical body, perhaps through intercessory prayer. In light of these new ways of thinking about consciousness, it no longer seems outrageous to suggest that prayer might act at a distance to bring about actual changes in the world.

In studies of intercessory prayer, researchers have found no correlation between the religious affiliation of the praying individual and the effects of prayer. This affirms the view that prayer is universal, that it belongs not just to a specific religion but to the entire human race. These findings sanction the importance of religious tolerance, asking us to honor the prayers and spiritual visions of other religious traditions, no matter how radically they may differ from our own.

Although personal religion does not correlate with prayer's effects in experimental studies, there is a quality that does make a great difference. It is a factor that sounds quite old-fashioned: *love*. Without love, the prayer experiments don't work as well; in fact, they often fall flat. As a physician, this finding intrigues me, because healers throughout history have uniformly proclaimed the importance of compassion, caring, and empathy for the patient. The best physicians I know honor the power of love and care in healing. They believe that, while penicillin may be powerful, penicillin plus love is more powerful still.

It is on these two issues in particular—the role of religious tolerance and the place of love and compassion in prayer—that I feel especially connected with Mother Teresa's work and writings. As Tony Stern points out in his introduction to this volume, Mother Teresa stated, "I've always said we should help a Hindu become a better Hindu, a Muslim become a better Muslim, a Catholic become a better Catholic."

There is a related story about Mother Teresa that attests to her tolerance, one that I have always adored, although it may be apocryphal. A brash young reporter once asked her, "Are you a saint?" Without hesitating, she poked the young man in the chest with a gnarled finger and said, "Yes, and so are you!"

Mother Teresa would undoubtedly insist that prayer does not need science to validate it, and I would agree. People test prayer every day in their lives, and life is the most important experimental laboratory of all. But, since science is one of the most powerful factors guiding modern life, we would be foolish to disregard what science has to say about prayer, particularly since so much of its current comments are positive.

One of the most remarkable trends in modern medicine is the return of prayer.[4] Three years ago, only three medical schools in the United States had courses exploring the role of religion and spiritual practice in health; currently, nearly thirty do.[5] First-rate researchers are examining the effects of prayer in healing at various medical schools, hospitals, and research institutions; national conferences linking spirituality and healthcare are becoming routine.

Somewhere, Mother Teresa must be smiling.

ENDNOTES

1. E.J. Larson, "Scientists are still keeping the faith," *Nature* (April 3, 1997): 345.
2. Larry Dossey, Healing Words: *The Power of Prayer and the Practice of Medicine* (San Francisco: HarperSanFrancisco, 1993).
3. Larry Dossey, "Emerging Theories" in *Be Careful What You Pray For* (San Francisco: HarperSanFrancisco, 1997): 190-92.
4. Larry Dossey, "The return of prayer," *Alternative Therapies* 3:6 (1997): 10ff.
5. Jeffrey S. Levin, David B. Larson, Christina M. Puchalski, "Religion and spirituality in medicine: research and education," *Journal of the American Medical Association* 278 (1997): 792-93.

Larry Dossey, M.D., is Executive Editor of *Alternative Therapies* and author of *Healing Words, Prayer Is Good Medicine,* and *Be Careful What You Pray For.*

Introduction

Anthony Stern, M.D.

The woman we all knew as Mother Teresa was devoutly Catholic and profoundly devoted to Jesus. She expressed her ceaseless devotion in so many ways, central among them her well-known work with the poor and the sick. Less known expressions included her deep respect for all religions and her burning wish for all people to come closer to God. It was with a longing to reach as many souls as possible that she wrote, "I've always said we should help a Hindu become a better Hindu, a Muslim become a better Muslim, a Catholic become a better Catholic." And it was with a practical recognition of what works that she declared, "Everything starts from prayer."

It is in this spirit that the following collection of Mother Teresa's sayings if offered. I've selected and arranged them from many of Mother Teresa's prior writings to give the widest possible access to people with no clear path as well as to those with various inner paths. I have tried to glean pearls of inspiration that provide an ecumenical entry into a life of prayer. And I've framed a host of Mother Teresa's reflections within this topic of prayer.

While Mother Teresa did not fully undertake an entirely universal approach herself, the basic direction she took was shown on the occasion she asked a wealthy person to build a mosque in Yemen, with the plea that the Muslim brothers and sisters there needed a place to meet God.

It is the same direction she took with one of her friends and biographers, Navin Chawla. She knew he was a non observant, nearly atheistic Hindu, yet not once over the years did she question his beliefs or his religion. But she did repeatedly, some might say incessantly, nudge him with the same question, "Have you begun to pray yet?"

Consider also one of the projects dearest to Mother Teresa's heart: her Homes for the Dying, where every person receives the last rites of his or her own tradition. She was overheard to whisper to one of the terminally ill, "You say a prayer in your religion, and I will say a prayer as I know it. Together we will say this prayer and it will be something beautiful for God." By the early 1980s, 17,000 people had died in these Homes. Seeing the peace and beauty of their deaths, she was sure that all these souls, whatever their faiths or sects, had gone straight to heaven.

For Mother Teresa, prayer was the universal way to God. Her own spiritual advisor and biographer Edward Le Joly drove this point home, observing that when a journalist approached her at an airport with the request, "Have you a message for the American people?" Mother Teresa didn't say "give more," or even "love one another more." Rather, she answered without hesitation, "Yes, they should pray more."

And so, let's be clear: The book you hold now gives the same answer by the same great spiritual leader and teacher, only in an extended form. Instead of her succinct response amidst the bustle of an airport, you have a set of meditations to be savored slowly in your home. It's a fuller, more developed version of the same basic counsel, the same basic plea: "Pray more."

Everything Starts from Prayer relates more directly to personal and private prayer than to ritual and community prayer. This is fitting, because everything depends on your own beginning. Praying as an individual is no substitute for for the spiritual nurturance, sharing, and guidance of communal practice and service. Yet we need to begin, again and again, on our own, digging within our own ground, making room for the grace that is always available to us. Our rote prayers and our prayers together can have great meaning as a pooling of devotional energies only when they're infused with the fire of individual souls—the sweet and profound energy our own sould release when they've caught fire.

When Dorothy Hunt was considering an idea that ultimately became the lovely Mother Teresa collection *Love: A Fruit Always in Season*, she asked permission to undertake the task. Mother Teresa's reply: "Make it a prayer." Make the very work a prayer. My one suggestion for reading this book is an echo of hers: Make it a prayer. The more seriously and openly you approach it, the more the words will penetrate. The more you bring your whole self to it with unhurried simplicity and receptivity, the more the thoughts and feelings behind the words will touch something deep inside you. And the more fully you connect with your own wish to be in the presence of the Eternal as you read, the more likely it will be that the holy meaning behind the words will spark something real in you.

In her wonderful book *A Simple Path*, Mother Teresa introduced readings from her Order's prayer book by suggesting that readers could replace "Jesus" with "God" in their prayers if they were not Christian. Similarly here, feel free to replace the word "God" with whatever works best for you in referring to a higher power in your life. The same should be urged for Mother Teresa's reference to God as "he" or "him," and of other traditional gender vocabulary herein. Please substitute words you find acceptable if these are off-putting in any way.

Mother Teresa spoke often of how utterly she relied on the power of prayer to connect her to God. Twenty-four hours a day, she'd say. And for emphasis, she sometimes added that if the day were longer, that's how much longer she'd need God's strength through prayer.

But then, what spiritual seeker has not depended on prayer? And what heart has not cried out, and not been better for having done so?

THE NEED TO PRAY

EVERYTHING STARTS FROM PRAYER. Without asking God for love, we cannot possess love and still less are we able to give it to others. Just as people today are speaking so much about the poor but they do not know the poor, we too cannot talk so much about prayer and yet not know how to pray.

The Need to Pray

You may be exhausted with work, you may even kill yourself, but unless your work is interwoven with love, it is useless. To work without love is slavery.

———

People throughout the world may look different or have a different religion, education, or position, but they are all the same. They are the people to be loved. They are all hungry for love.

I N MOST MODERN ROOMS YOU SEE AN
electrical light that can be turned on
by a switch. But, if there is no connection
with the main power house, then there
can be no light. Faith and prayer is the
connection with God, and when that is
there, there is service.

The Need
to Pray

3

WE HAVE TO POSSESS BEFORE WE CAN give. He who has the mission of giving to others must grow first in the knowledge of God. He must be full of that knowledge.

———

TO BE ABLE TO GIVE, YOU MUST HAVE.

LOVE TO BE TRUE HAS TO BEGIN WITH God in prayer. If we pray, we will be able to love, and if we love, we will be able to serve.

———

WHATEVER RELIGION WE ARE, WE MUST pray together. Children need to learn to pray and they need to have their parents pray with them.

IT IS EASY TO LOVE THE PEOPLE FAR AWAY. It is not always easy to love those close to us. It is easier to give a cup of rice to relieve hunger than to relieve the loneliness and pain of someone unloved in our own home. Bring love into your own home for this is where our love for each other must start.

IN ONE OF THE HOUSES OUR SISTERS visited, a woman had been dead a long time before anyone knew it, and then they found out only because her corpse had begun to rot. Her neighbors didn't even know her name.

———

THERE IS MUCH SUFFERING IN THE world—very much. And this material suffering is suffering from hunger, suffering from homelessness, from all kinds of diseases, but I still think the greatest suffering is being lonely, feeling unloved, just having no one.

The Need
to Pray

7

THERE ARE DIFFERENT KINDS OF POVERTY.
In India some people live and die in
hunger.

But in the West you have another kind of
poverty, spiritual poverty. This is far worse.
People do not believe in God, do not pray.
People do not care for each other. You have
the poverty of people who are dissatisfied
with what they have, who do not know
how to suffer, who give in to despair.
This poverty of heart is often more
difficult to relieve and to defeat.

I REMEMBER SOME TIME AGO I VISITED a very wonderful home for old people. There were about forty there and they had everything, but they were all looking towards the door. There was not a smile on their faces, and I asked the sister in charge of them, "Sister, why are these people not smiling? Why are they looking towards the door?" And she, very beautifully, had to answer and give the truth: "It's the same every day. They are longing for someone to come and visit them."

This is great poverty.

WHEN THINGS BECOME OUR MASTERS, we are very poor.

You and I have been created for greater things. We have not been created to just pass through this life without aim. And that greater aim is to love and be loved.

SOME CALL HIM ISHWAR, SOME CALL him Allah, some simply God, but we all have to acknowledge that it is He who made us for greater things: to love and be loved. What matters is that we love. We cannot love without prayer, and so whatever religion we are we must pray together.

You will find Calcutta all over the world if you have eyes to see. The streets of Calcutta lead to every man's door. I know that you may want to make a trip to Calcutta, but it is easy to love people far away. It is not always easy to love people who live beside us. What about the ones I dislike or look down upon?

———

It is easy to be proud and harsh and selfish—so easy. But we have been created for better things.

ONCE IN A WHILE WE SHOULD ASK ourselves several questions in order to guide our actions. We should ask questions like: Do I know the poor? Do I know, in the first place, the poor in my family, those who are closest to me—people who are poor, but not because they lack bread?

There are other types of poverty just as painful because they are more intrinsic.

Perhaps what my husband or wife lacks, what my children lack, what my parents lack, is not clothes or food. Perhaps they lack love, because I do not give it to them!

WHERE DOES LOVE BEGIN?
In our own homes.
When does it begin?
When we pray together.

WE HAVE TO FEED OURSELVES.
We can die of spiritual starvation.
We must be filled continually, like a
machine. When one little thing in the
machine is not working, then the whole
machine is not working properly.

I AM ASKED WHAT IS ONE TO DO TO BE sure one is following the way of salvation. I answer: "Love God. And, above all, pray."

2

STARTING WITH SILENCE

I T IS VERY HARD TO PRAY IF ONE DOES not know how. We must help ourselves to learn. The most important thing is silence.

———

W E NEED TO FIND GOD AND GOD cannot be found in noise and restlessness.

WE CANNOT PLACE OURSELVES
directly in God's presence
without imposing upon ourselves
interior and exterior silence.
That is why we must accustom ourselves
to stillness of the soul,
of the eyes,
of the tongue.

T HERE IS NO LIFE OF PRAYER
without silence.

———

E VERYTHING BEGINS WITH PRAYER
that is born in the silence of our
hearts.

I F WE REALLY WANT TO PRAY, WE MUST first learn to listen: for in the silence of the heart God speaks.

———

S ILENCE OF THE *HEART*, NOT ONLY OF the mouth—that too is necessary.
Then you can hear God everywhere:
in the closing of the door,
in the person who needs you,
in the birds that sing,
in the flowers, the animals—
that silence which is wonder and praise.

THE CONTEMPLATIVES AND ASCETICS of all ages and religions have sought God in the silence and solitude of the desert, forest, and mountain.

———

WE TOO ARE CALLED TO WITHDRAW at certain intervals into deeper silence and aloneness with God, together as a community as well as personally. To be alone with him, not with our books, thoughts, and memories but completely stripped of everything, to dwell lovingly in his presence—silent, empty, expectant, and motionless.

Starting
with Silence

L ISTEN IN SILENCE, BECAUSE IF YOUR heart is full of other things you cannot hear the voice of God. But when you have listened to the voice of God in the stillness of your heart, then your heart is filled with God. This will need much sacrifice, but if we really mean to pray and want to pray we must be ready to do it now.

ah:

To foster and maintain a prayerful atmosphere of exterior silence we shall

~ respect certain times and places of more strict silence

~ move about and work prayerfully, quietly and gently

~ avoid at all costs all unnecessary speaking and notice

~ speak, when we have to, softly, gently, saying just what is necessary

~ look forward to profound silence as a holy and precious time, a withdrawal into the living silence of God.

W E NEED SILENCE TO BE ALONE
with God, to speak to him, to
listen to him, to ponder his words deep
in our hearts. We need to be alone with
God in silence to be renewed and to
be transformed. Silence gives us a new
outlook on life. In it we are filled with
the grace of God himself, which makes
us do all things with joy.

IF WE ARE CAREFUL OF SILENCE
it will be easy to pray.
There is so much talk,
so much repetition,
so much carrying on
of tales in words and in writing.
Our prayer life suffers so much
because our hearts are not silent.

L OOKING AT YOUR EYES
I can tell whether there is peace
in your heart or not.

We see people radiating joy,
and in their eyes you can see purity. If we
want our minds to have silence, keep a
silence of the eyes. Use your two eyes to
help you to pray better.

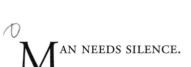

M AN NEEDS SILENCE.

To be alone or together looking for
God in silence.

There it is that we accumulate the
inward power which we distribute
in action, put in the smallest duty
and spend in the severest hardships
that befall us.

Silence came before creation,
and the heavens were spread
without a word.

INTERIOR SILENCE IS VERY DIFFICULT
but we must make the effort. In silence
we will find new energy and true unity.
The energy of God will be ours to do all
things well.

———

THESE ARE ONLY THE FIRST STEPS
toward prayer, but if we never
make the first step with determination,
we will not reach the last one:
the presence of God.

I F YOU SINCERELY WANT TO LEARN to pray: keep silence.

3

LIKE A LITTLE CHILD

M Y SECRET IS A VERY SIMPLE ONE:
I pray.

P RAYER IS SIMPLY TALKING TO GOD.
He speaks to us: we listen.
We speak to him: he listens.
A two-way process:
speaking and listening.

That is really prayer.
Both sides listening
and both sides speaking.

Start and end the day with prayer. Come to God as a child. If you find it hard to pray you can say, "Come Holy Spirit, guide me, protect me, clear out my mind so that I can pray."

WHEREVER THEY ARE,
the Missionaries of Charity
start the day's work with the same
prayer from their community
prayer book:

Dear Lord, the Great Healer, I kneel
before you, since every perfect gift
must come from you. I pray, give skill
to my hands, clear vision to my mind,
kindness and meekness to my heart.
Give me singleness of purpose, strength
to lift up a part of the burden of my
suffering fellowmen, and a realization
of the privilege that is mine. Take from
my heart all guile and worldliness, that
with the simple faith of a child, I may
rely on you.
Amen.

HOW DO YOU PRAY?
You should go to God like a little child. A child has no difficulty expressing his mind in simple words that say so much.

If a child is not yet spoiled and has not yet learned to tell lies, he will tell everything. This is what I mean by being childlike.

HOW DO WE LEARN TO PRAY? By praying. It is very hard to pray if one does not know how. We must help ourselves to learn. Pray with absolute trust in God's loving care for you and let him fill you with joy that you may preach without preaching.

Y OU CAN PRAY ANYTIME, ANYWHERE.
You do not have to be in a chapel
or a church.

L OVE TO PRAY—FEEL THE NEED
to pray often during the day and take
the trouble to pray. If you want
to pray better, you must pray more.

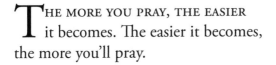

THE MORE YOU PRAY, THE EASIER
it becomes. The easier it becomes,
the more you'll pray.

———

YOU CAN PRAY WHILE YOU WORK.
Work doesn't stop prayer and
prayer doesn't stop work. It requires
only that small raising of the mind to
him:
"I love you God, I trust you,
I believe in you, I need you now."
Small things like that.
They are wonderful prayers.

Like a
Little
Child

41

OFTEN, UNDER THE PRETEXT
of humility, of trust, of
abandonment, we can forget
to use the strength of our will.
Everything depends on these words:
"I will" or "I will not."
And into the expression "I will"
I must put all my energy.

———

WE MUST KNOW THE MEANING
of the prayers we say and feel
the sweetness of each word to make these
prayers of great profit; we must sometimes
meditate on them and often during the
day find our rest in them.

YOU CAN SAY, "MY LORD, I LOVE YOU."
"My God, I am sorry."
"My God, I believe in You."
"My God, I trust You."
"Help us to love one
another as You love us."

YOU CAN PRAY FOR THE WORKS
of others and help them.
For example, in our community there
are second self helpers who offer their
prayers for a sister who needs the strength
to carry on her active work. And we also
have the contemplative sisters and brothers,
who pray for us all the time.

Like a
Little
Child

"I KEPT THE LORD EVER BEFORE MY EYES because he is ever at my right hand that I may not slip," says the psalmist. God is within me with a more intimate presence than that whereby I am in myself: in him we live and move and have our being. It is he who gives life to all, that gives power and being to all that exists. But for his sustaining presence, all things would cease to be and fall back into nothingness.

———

CONSIDER THAT YOU ARE IN GOD, surrounded and encompassed by God, swimming in God.

WE NEED TO HELP EACH OTHER in our prayers. Let us free our minds. Let's not pray long, drawn-out prayers, but let's pray short ones full of love. Let us pray on behalf of those who do not pray. Let us remember, if we want to be able to love, we must be able to pray!

750 YRS

IT IS NOW SEVEN HUNDRED AND FIFTY YEARS since St. Francis of Assisi composed the following prayer for himself and for those whom he taught to love God:

Lord, make me an instrument of your peace.
Where there is hatred, let me sow love.
Where there is injury, let me sow pardon.
Where there is friction, let me sow union.
Where there is error, let me sow truth.
Where there is doubt, let me sow faith.
Where there is despair, let me sow hope.
Where there is darkness, let me sow light.
Where there is sadness, let me sow joy.

O Divine Master, grant that I may not so much seek
To be consoled as to console,
To be understood as to understand,
To be loved as to love,
For it is in giving that we receive.
It is in pardoning that we are pardoned.
It is in dying that we are born to eternal life.

WE WANT SO MUCH TO PRAY properly and then we fail. We get discouraged and give up on prayer. God allowed the failure but he did not want the discouragement. He wants us to be more childlike, more humble, more grateful in prayer.

Key

Try speaking directly to God.
Just speak. Tell him everything,
talk to him. He is our father, he is
father to us all whatever religion
we are. We have to put our trust
in him and love him, believe in him,
work for him. And if we pray, we
will get all the answers we need.

***

Let God use you without consulting
you: "You, Lord, only You, all of You;
make use of me."

ONE OF MY FAVORITE DEVOTIONAL songs is called *Only a Shadow*. Its verses run like this:

> The love I have for you, my Lord
> Is only a shadow of your love for me,
> Your deep abiding love.
> My own belief in you, my Lord,
> Is only a shadow of your faith in me,
> Your deep and trusting faith.
> My life is in your hands.
> My love for you will grow, my Lord.
> Your light in me will shine.
> The dream I have today, my Lord,
> Is only a shadow of your dream for me,
> If I but follow you.
> The joy I feel today, my Lord,
> Is only a shadow of your joys for me,
> Only a shadow of all that will be
> When we meet face to face.

Like a
Little
Child

49

THERE ARE SOME PEOPLE WHO, in order not to pray, use as an excuse the fact that life is so hectic that it prevents them from praying.

This cannot be.

Prayer does not demand that we interrupt our work, but that we continue working as if it were a prayer.

It is not necessary to always be meditating, nor to consciously experience the sensation that we are talking to God, no matter how nice this would be. What matters is being with him, living in him, in his will.

G OD IS PURITY HIMSELF; NOTHING impure can come before him, but I don't think God can hate, because God is love and God loves us in spite of our misery.

God loves because he is love, but impurity is an obstacle to seeing God.

OUR SOULS SHOULD BE LIKE A transparent crystal through which God can be perceived.

———

OUR CRYSTAL IS SOMETIMES COVERED with dirt and dust. To remove this dust we carry out an examination of our conscience in order to obtain a clean heart. God will help us to remove that dust, as long as we allow him to: if that is our will, his will comes about.

THE MORE WE EMPTY OURSELVES,
the more room we give God to fill us.

———

WHEN WE HAVE NOTHING TO GIVE,
let us give him that nothingness.

Like a
Little
Child

R ICHES, MATERIAL OR SPIRITUAL, can suffocate you if they are not used in the right way. Remain as "empty" as possible, so that God can fill you.

———

E VEN GOD CANNOT PUT ANYTHING into what is already full. He does not impose himself on us.

I T IS NOT HOW MUCH WE REALLY HAVE to give but how empty we are—so that we can receive fully in our life. Take away your eyes from yourself and rejoice that you have nothing—that you are nothing—that you can do nothing.

WE HAVE TO PRAY ON BEHALF
of those who do not pray.

WE SHOULD BE PROFESSIONALS
in prayer.

L OVE TO PRAY. FEEL OFTEN DURING the day the need for prayer and take trouble to pray. God is always speaking to us. Listen to him.

———

R ECREATION IS A MEANS TO PRAY better. Relaxation sweeps away the cobwebs of the mind.

WHEN YOU PRAY, GIVE THANKS to God for all his gifts because everything is his and a gift from him.

———

YOUR SOUL IS A GIFT OF GOD.

A S LONG AS WE DO NOT MAKE
the best effort we are capable
of, we cannot feel discouraged by
our failures. We cannot claim any
successes either. We should give
God all the credit and be extremely
sincere when we do so.

B E SINCERE IN YOUR PRAYERS.
Do you pray your prayers?
Do you know how to pray?
Do you love to pray?
Sincerity is nothing but humility and
you acquire humility only by accepting
humiliations.

Like a
Little
Child

ALL THAT HAS BEEN SAID ABOUT humility is not enough to teach you humility. All that you have read about humility is not enough to teach you humility. You learn humility only by accepting humiliations. And you will meet humiliation all through your lives.

———

THE GREATEST HUMILIATION IS TO know that you are nothing. This you come to know when you face God in prayer. When you come face to face with God, you cannot but know that you are nothing, that you have nothing.

I F WE REALLY FULLY BELONG TO GOD, then we must be at his disposal and we must trust in him. We must never be preoccupied with the future. There is no reason to be so. God is there.

———

Y ESTERDAY IS GONE. Tomorrow has not yet come. We have only today.

Let us begin.

DON'T SEARCH FOR GOD IN FAR LANDS—
he is not there. He is close to you. He
is with you. Just keep the lamp burning and
you will always see him. Watch and pray.
Keep kindling the lamp and you will see his
love and you will see how sweet is the Lord
you love.

———

TODAY, MORE THAN EVER, WE NEED
to pray for the light to know the
will of God, for the love to accept the will
of God, for the way to do the will of God.

PRAY LOVINGLY LIKE CHILDREN,
with an earnest desire to love
much and make loved the love
that is not loved.

Let us thank God for all his love for us,
in so many ways and in so many places.

———

MAY GOD GIVE US ALL OPENNESS
to ways leading beyond our
own selves.

P RAYER, TO BE FRUITFUL, MUST COME
from the heart and must be able to
touch the heart of God.

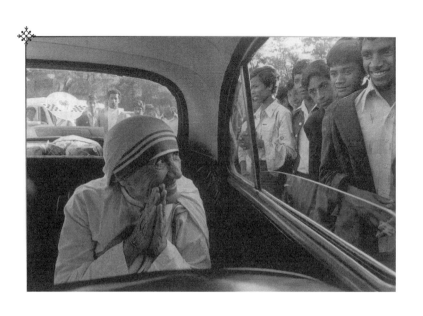

4

OPENING YOUR HEART

OPEN YOUR HEARTS
to the love of God which
he will give you. He loves you with
tenderness. And he will give you not
to keep but to share.

OUR PRAYERS SHOULD BE BURNING words coming forth from the furnace of hearts filled with love. In your prayers, speak to God with great reverence and confidence.

D<small>O NOT DRAG BEHIND OR</small> run ahead; do not shout or keep silent, but devoutly, with great sweetness, with natural simplicity, without any affectation, offer your praise to God with the whole of your heart and soul.

WE OUGHT EVERY DAY TO RENEW
our resolution and to rouse
ourselves to fervor, as if it were the first
day of our conversion, saying, "Help
me, Lord God, in my good resolve
and in thy holy service, and give me
grace this very day really and truly to
begin, for what I have done till now is
nothing."

THE PRAYER THAT COMES FROM THE mind and heart and which we do not read in books is called mental prayer. In vocal prayer we speak to God; in mental prayer he speaks to us. It is then that God pours himself into us.

MENTAL PRAYER IS GREATLY FOSTERED by simplicity—that is, forgetfulness of self by transcending of the body and of our senses, and by frequent aspirations that feed our prayer. "In mental prayer," says Saint John Vianney, "shut your eyes, shut your mouth, and open your heart."

PRAYER ENLARGES THE HEART UNTIL it is capable of containing God's gift of himself. Ask and seek and your heart will grow big enough to receive him and keep him as your own.

———

OFFER TO GOD EVERY WORD YOU SAY, every movement you make. We must more and more fall in love with God.

WE NEED PRAYERS IN ORDER TO better carry out the work of God, and so that in every moment we may know how to be completely available to him.

We should make every effort to walk in the presence of God, to see God in all the persons we meet, to live our prayer throughout the day.

———

WE MUST PRAY PERSEVERINGLY and with great love.

LOVE IS A FRUIT IN SEASON at all times and within the reach of every hand. Anyone may gather it and no limit is set. Everyone can reach this love through meditation, the spirit of prayer and sacrifice, by an intense inner life.

Do we really live this life?

Opening
Your
Heart

L OVING SHOULD BE AS NORMAL
to us as living and breathing,
day after day until our death.

———

A M I A DARK LIGHT? A FALSE LIGHT?
A bulb without the connection,
therefore shedding no radiance?

Put your heart into being a bright
light.

IT IS NOT WHAT WE DO OR HOW MUCH we do, but how much love we put into the action because that action is our love for God in action.

G OD SPEAKS IN THE SILENCE
of our heart, and we listen.
And then we speak to God from the
fullness of our heart, and God listens.

———

E VEN WHEN WE SIN OR MAKE A
mistake, let's allow that to help
us grow closer to God. Let's tell him
humbly, "I know I shouldn't have done
this, but even this failure I offer to
you."

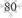

O<small>UR WORDS ARE USELESS UNLESS</small> they come from the bottom of the heart.

G<small>IVE YOURSELF FULLY TO</small> G<small>OD</small>. He will use you to accomplish great things on the condition that you believe much more in his love than in your weakness.

Opening
Your
Heart

81

IS MY HEART SO CLEAN THAT I CAN SEE the face of God in my brother, my sister who is that black one, that white one, that naked one, that one suffering from leprosy, that dying one?

And this is what we must pray for.

———

GOD DWELLS IN US. That's what gives him a beautiful power. It doesn't matter where you are as long as you are clean of heart. Clean of heart means openness, that complete freedom, that detachment that allows you to love God without hindrance, without obstacles.

EVERY NIGHT BEFORE YOU GO TO BED you must make an examination of conscience (because you don't know if you will be alive in the morning!). Whatever is troubling you, or whatever wrong you may have done, you need to repair it. For example, if you have stolen something, then try to give it back.

I F YOU HAVE HURT SOMEBODY, try to make up to that person; do it directly. If you cannot make up like that, at least then make up with God by saying, "I'm very sorry." This is important because just as we have acts of love, we also must have acts of contrition. You could say, "Lord, I'm sorry for having offended you and I promise you I will try not to offend you again."

I T FEELS GOOD TO BE FREE OF BURDENS, to have a clean heart. Remember that God is merciful, he is the merciful father to us all. We are his children and he will forgive and forget if we remember to do so.

———

E XAMINE YOUR HEART FIRST, though, to see if there is any lack of forgiveness of others still inside, because how can we ask God for forgiveness if we cannot forgive others?

P EOPLE ASK ME WHAT ADVICE I HAVE
for a married couple struggling in
their relationship. I always answer "Pray
and forgive;" and to young people who
come from violent homes, "Pray and
forgive;" and to the single mother with
no family support, "Pray and forgive."

REMEMBER, IF YOU TRULY REPENT, if you really mean it with a clean heart, you will be absolved in God's eyes. He will forgive you if you truly confess. So pray to be able to forgive those who have hurt you or whom you don't like, and forgive as you have been forgiven.

Opening
Your
Heart

PRAYER IS A JOY.
Prayer is the sunshine of God's
love, prayer is hope of eternal happiness,
prayer is the burning flame of God's love for
you and for me. Let us pray for each other,
for this is the best way to love
one another.

———

TODAY BE THE SUNSHINE OF GOD'S LOVE.

GOD IS STILL LOVE,
he is still loving the world.
Today God loves the world so much
that he gives you and he gives me to
love the world, to be his love and
compassion.

———

YOU MAY BE EXHAUSTED WITH WORK,
even kill yourself, but unless your
work is interwoven with love, it is useless.

———

WE MUST ALL FILL OUR HEARTS
with great love. Don't imagine
that love, to be true and burning,
must be extraordinary.

GOD LOVES EACH ONE OF US WITH
a most tender and personal love.
His longing for me is dearer than
my longing for him.

———

THERE IS NO LIMIT TO GOD'S LOVE.
It is without limit and its depth
cannot be sounded.

THE BEST WAY TO SHOW YOUR
gratitude to God and people is
to accept everything with joy. A joyful
heart is the normal result of a heart
burning with love.

———

IT IS SO EASY TO BE PROUD, HARSH,
moody and selfish, but we have been
created for greater things; why stoop
down to things that will spoil the
beauty of our hearts?

IN THE SILENCE OF THE HEART God speaks.

What does God say to us? He says: "I have called you by your name, you are mine; water will not drown you, fire will not burn you, I will give up nations for you, you are precious to me, I love you. Even if a mother could forget her child, I will not forget you. I have carved you in the palm of my hand."

W E CANNOT SPEAK UNLESS WE HAVE
listened, unless we have made our
connection with God. From the fullness
of the heart, the mouth will speak,
the mind will think.

J UST ONCE, LET THE LOVE OF GOD
take entire and absolute possession
of your heart; let it become to your
heart like a second nature; let your
heart suffer nothing contrary to enter;
let it apply itself continually to increase
this love of God by seeking to please
him in all things and refusing him
nothing; let it accept as from his
hand everything that happens to it;
let it have a firm determination never
to commit any fault deliberately and
knowingly or, if it should fail, to be
humbled and to rise up again at once—
and such a heart will pray continually.

5
ENDING IN SILENCE

S OULS OF PRAYER ARE SOULS OF GREAT
silence.

———

S ILENCE IS THE BEAUTIFUL FRUIT
of prayer. We must learn not only
the silence of the mouth but also
the silence of the heart,
of the eyes,
of the ears
and of the mind,
which I call the five silences.

G OD IS THE FRIEND OF SILENCE. See how nature—trees, flowers, grass—grows in silence. See the stars, the moon and the sun, how they move in silence.

———

I N THAT SILENCE, HE WILL LISTEN TO US; there he will speak to our soul, and there we will hear his voice.

THE FRUIT OF SILENCE IS FAITH.
The fruit of faith is prayer.
The fruit of prayer is love.
The fruit of love is service.
And the fruit of service is silence.

Iᴺ ᴛʜᴇ ѕɪʟᴇɴᴄᴇ ᴏꜰ ᴛʜᴇ ʜᴇᴀʀᴛ Gᴏᴅ speaks. If you face God in prayer and silence, God will speak to you. Then you will know that you are nothing. It is only when you realize your nothingness, your emptiness, that God can fill you with himself.

Ending
in
Silence

S ILENCE GIVES US A NEW WAY
of looking at everything.
We need this silence in order
to touch souls.

———

G OD IS THE FRIEND OF SILENCE.
His language is silence.
"Be still and know that I am God."

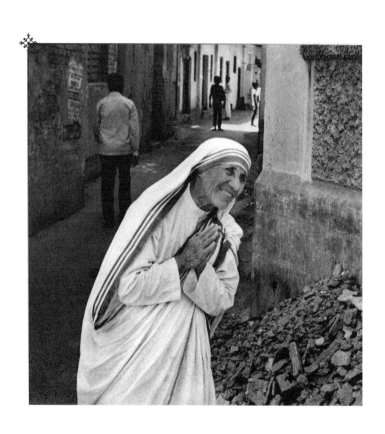

6

THE FRUIT OF PRAYER

THE MORE WE RECEIVE IN SILENT PRAYER, the more we can give in our active life.

———

THE ESSENTIAL THING IS NOT WHAT WE say, but what God says to us and through us.

All our words will be useless unless they come from within.

———

YOU CAN DO WHAT I CAN'T DO. I can do what you can't do. Together we can do something beautiful for God.

G OD DOES NOT DEMAND
that I be successful.
God demands that I be faithful.

When facing God, results are not
important. Faithfulness is what is
important.

———

W E DO NOT STRIVE FOR SPECTACULAR
actions. What counts is the gift of
yourself, the degree of love you put into
each of your deeds.

———

W E CAN DO NO GREAT THINGS—
only small things with great love.

T HE FRUIT OF PRAYER IS A DEEPENING
of faith.

———

B E FAITHFUL IN SMALL THINGS BECAUSE
it is in them that your strength lies.

P RAYER FEEDS THE SOUL—
as blood is to the body,
prayer is to the soul—and
it brings you closer to God.

—

W HEN YOU BECOME FULL OF GOD,
you will do all your work well,
all of it wholeheartedly. And when you are
full of God, you will do everything well.
This you can do only if you pray,
if you know how to pray, if you love
prayer, and if you pray well.

THE MORE I GO AROUND,
the better I understand how
very necessary it is for us to pray
the work, to make the work
our love for God in action.

———

GOD MAY ALLOW EVERYTHING TO GO
upside down in the hands of a very
talented and capable person. Unless the
work is interwoven with love, it is useless.

L OVE IS NOT SOMETHING
that fossilizes, but something
that lives. Works of love, and declaring
love, is the way to peace. And where
does this love begin?
Right in our own hearts.
We must know that we have been
created for greater things, not just
to be a number in the world,
not just to go for diplomas and degrees,
this work and that work.

We have been created in order
to love and be loved.

IF WE NEGLECT PRAYER AND IF THE BRANCH is not connected with the vine, it will die. That connecting of the branch to the vine is prayer. If that connection is there then love is there, then joy is there, and we will be the sunshine of God's love, the hope of eternal happiness, the flame of burning love.

This is the true reason for our existence: to be the sunshine of God's love, to be the hope of eternal happiness. That's all.

THE FRUIT OF PRAYER IS A CLEAN HEART
and a clean heart is free to love.

———

WHEN YOU HAVE A CLEAN HEART
it means you are open and honest
with God, you are not hiding anything
from him, and this lets him take what
he wants from you.

THE ENERGY OF GOD WILL BE OURS
to do all things well, and so will the
unity of our thoughts with his thoughts,
the unity of our prayers with his prayers,
the unity of our actions with his actions,
of our life with his life.
Unity is the fruit of prayer,
of humility, of love.

———

THE VALUE OF OUR ACTIONS
corresponds exactly to the
value of the prayer we make.

NEVER THINK THAT A SMALL ACTION done to your neighbor is not worth much. It is not how much we do that is pleasing to God, but how much love we put into the doing.

Make sure you know your neighbor, for that knowledge will lead you to great love and love to personal service.

The
Fruit of
Prayer

WE IMPATIENTLY AWAIT GOD'S PARADISE,
but we have in our hands the power
to be in paradise right here and now.
Being happy with God means this:
to love as he loves,
to help as he helps,
to give as he gives,
to serve as he serves.

LOVE ACCEPTS ALL AND GIVES ALL.
Love should be as natural as living
and breathing.

IN THE SILENCE OF THE HEART,
God speaks and you have to listen.
Then in the fullness of your heart,
because it is full of God,
full of love,
full of compassion,
full of faith,
your mouth will speak.

The
Fruit of
Prayer

119

YOU MAY BE WRITING, AND THE FULLNESS of your heart will come to your hand also. Your heart may speak through writing. Your heart may speak through your eyes also. You know that when you look at people they must be able to see God in your eyes. If you get distracted and worldly, then they will not be able to see God like that. The fullness of our heart is expressed in our eyes, in our touch, in what we write, in what we say, in the way we walk, the way we receive, the way we need. That is the fullness of our heart expressing itself in many different ways.

WE DO NOT ROAM, BUT WE CULTIVATE
the vagabond spirit of abandonment.
We have nothing to live on,
yet we live splendidly;
nothing to walk on,
yet we walk fearlessly;
nothing to lean on,
but yet we lean on God confidently;
for we are his own and he is our provident
father.

———

WE ARE CALLED UPON NOT TO BE
successful, but to be faithful.

The
Fruit of
Prayer

121

WE GET SO MANY VISITORS EVERY DAY at Mother House in Calcutta. When I meet them I give each one my "business card." On it is written: *The fruit of prayer is faith; The fruit of faith is love; The fruit of love is service; The fruit of service is peace.*

This is very good "business!"

A T THE HOME FOR THE DYING
in Kalighat, a visitor wondered
at the peace that pervaded everywhere.
I said simply: "God is here.
Castes and creeds mean nothing.
It does not matter that they are not
of my faith."

WE OURSELVES FEEL THAT WHAT WE
are doing is just a drop in the ocean.
But if that drop was not there, I think the
ocean would be less by that missing drop.
We don't have to think in numbers.

We can only love one person at a time,
serve one person at a time.

WHEREVER GOD HAS PUT YOU,
that is your vocation.
It is not what we do but how
much love we put into it.

———

TO THE CAST OF A MUSICAL PERFORMANCE
in Calcutta, I said: "Your work and our
work complete each other. What we are
doing is needed in the world as never before.
You are giving them joy by your action
and we are doing the same by service.
And it is the same action whether you
are singing and dancing and we are
rubbing and scrubbing. You are filling the
world with the love God has given you."

The
Fruit of
Prayer

J OY SHOWS FROM THE EYES,
it appears when one speaks and walks.
It cannot be kept closed inside us.
It reacts outside.
When people find in your eyes
that habitual happiness,
they will understand that
they are the beloved children of God.

WE ARE TALKING ABOUT THE JOY
that comes from union with God,
from living in his presence, because living
in his presence fills us with joy.

When I speak of joy, I do not identify
it with loud laughter or with noise.
This is not true happiness.
Sometimes it hides other things.

When I speak of happiness,
I refer to an inner and deep peace,
which shows itself in our eyes,
on our faces, in our attitudes,
in our gestures, in our promptness.

The
Fruit of
Prayer

127

T HAT IS WHAT I SEE HAPPENING:
people coming to meet each other
because of their need for God.
The wonderful thing about it is that
there is a religious atmosphere;
they all speak about God.

This is a great experience for me.
I feel that to bring all these people
together to talk about God is really
wonderful. A new hope for the world.

THERE IS A TREMENDOUS STRENGTH that is growing in the world through this continual sharing, praying together, suffering together and working together.

———

WE DO NOTHING. He does everything. All glory must be returned to him.

God has not called me to be successful. He called me to be faithful.

ONE DAY IN CALCUTTA A MAN CAME with a prescription and said, "My only child is dying and this medicine can be brought only from outside of India." Just at that time, while we were still talking, a man came with a basket of medicine. Right on the top of that basket, there was this medicine.

If it had been inside, I would not have seen it. If he had come before, or if he had come afterward, I could not have seen it. But just at that time, out of the millions and millions of children in the world, God in his tenderness was concerned with this little child of the slums of Calcutta enough to send, just at that time, that amount of medicine to save that child.

I praise the tenderness and the love of God, because every little one, in a poor family or a rich family, is a child of God, created by the Creator of all things.

L ET US THANK GOD FOR ALL HIS LOVE for us, in so many ways and in so many places.

Let us in return, as an act of gratitude and adoration, determine to love him.

HOLINESS IS NOT A LUXURY FOR THE FEW;
it is not just for some people.
It is meant for you and for me, for all of us.
It is a simple duty, because if we learn to
love, we learn to be holy.

———

WE ALL HAVE MUCH TO GIVE, TO SHARE,
to contribute wherever we find
ourselves to be living.

Holiness starts in the home, by loving God
and those around us for his sake.

Total surrender to God must come in small details just as it comes in big details. It's nothing but that single word, "Yes, I accept whatever you give, and I give whatever you take." And this is just a simple way for us to be holy.

We must not create difficulties in our own minds. To be holy doesn't mean to do extraordinary things, to understand big things, but it is a simple acceptance, because I have given myself to God, because I belong to him—my total surrender. He could put me here. He could put me there. He can use me. He cannot use me. It doesn't matter because I belong so totally to him that he can do just what he wants to do with me.

M AKE SURE THAT YOU LET GOD'S GRACE
work in your souls by accepting
whatever he gives you, and giving him
whatever he takes from you. True holiness
consists in doing God's will with a smile.

———

O UR PROGRESS IN HOLINESS DEPENDS
on God and on ourselves—on God's
grace and on our will to be holy. We must
have a real living determination to reach
holiness.

WE MUST NOT ATTEMPT TO CONTROL God's actions. We must not count the stages in the journey he would have us make. We must not desire a clear perception of our advance along the road, nor know precisely where we are on the way of holiness.

———

BECOME HOLY. EACH ONE OF US has a capacity to become holy and the way to holiness is prayer.

WE TREAT ALL PEOPLE AS CHILDREN OF GOD. They are our brothers and sisters. We show great respect to them. Our work is to encourage these people, Christians as well as non-Christians, to do works of love. Every work of love done with a full heart brings people closer to God.

EVERY HUMAN BEING COMES from the hand of God, and we all know what is the love of God for us.

God has his own ways and means to work in the hearts of men and we do not know how close they are to him but by their actions we will always know whether they are at his disposal or not. Whether you are a Hindu, a Muslim or a Christian, how you live your life is the proof that you are fully his or not.

L OVING MUST BE AS NORMAL TO US
as living and breathing, day after day
until our death. To understand this and
practice it we need much prayer,
the kind that unites us with God
and overflows continually upon others.

———

O UR WORKS OF CHARITY ARE NOTHING
but the overflow of our love of God
from within. Therefore, the one who is
most united to him loves her neighbor most.

L ET NO ONE GLORY IN THEIR SUCCESS
but refer all to God in deepest
thankfulness; on the other hand,
no failure should dishearten them
as long as they have done their best.
God sees only our love.
God will not ask how
many books we have read,
how many miracles we have worked,
but whether we have done our best
for the love of him.
Have we played well?
Slept well?
Eaten well?
Nothing is small for God.

WE ARE SO SMALL
we look at things in a small way.
But God, being Almighty, sees everything
great. Therefore, even if you write a letter
for a blind man or you just go and
sit and listen,
or you take the mail for him,
or you visit somebody
or bring a flower to somebody
—small things—or wash clothes
for somebody,
or clean the house.
Very humble work, that is where
you and I must be.
For there are many people
who can do big things.
But there are very few people
who will do the small things.

IT IS SO BEAUTIFUL THAT WE COMPLETE each other! What we are doing in the slums, maybe you cannot do.
What you are doing in the level where you are called—in your family life, in your college life, in your work —we cannot do.
But you and we together are doing something beautiful for God.

OFTEN YOU SEE SMALL AND BIG WIRES,
new and old, cheap and expensive
electric cables. Alone they are useless and
until the current passes through them
there will be no light.
The wire is you and me.
The current is God.

———

WE HAVE THE POWER
to let the current pass through us
and use us to produce the light of the world
or we can refuse to be used and allow the
darkness to spread.

I F YOU HAVE LEARNED HOW TO PRAY,
then I am not afraid for you.
If you know how to pray, then you
will love prayer—and if you love to pray,
then you will pray. Knowledge will lead to
love and love to service.

———

A MONG YOURSELVES YOU CAN SHARE
your own experience of your need
to pray, and how you found prayer,
and what the fruit of prayer has been
in your own lives.

The
Fruit of
Prayer

143

L ET US SPREAD THE GOOD NEWS
that prayer is our strength.

Retreat Resources

Mother Teresa advocates taking periods of time away from one's routine, even one's regular spiritual routine, to develop and renew a life of prayer. Perhaps the best place to begin looking for retreats is by asking local friends, family members, spiritual advisors, or trusted community leaders what ones they may be able to suggest.

Sometimes people need to travel far and wide to find where they're going. Here are a few places you can contact as further resources; needless to say, using Google or another search engine can lead you to a lot more information about these centers.

1) Contemplative Outreach National Office (Butler, NJ)—an outgrowth of the "Centering Prayer" movement, and particularly Father Thomas Keating's work. Primarily Catholic in its roots, but open to others. Phone: 973-838-3384.

2) Pendle Hill (Wallingford, PA)—a Quaker retreat center with a strong inter-faith history. Phone: 800-742-3150.

3) Shalem Institute (Bethesda, MD)—an ecumenical Christian center founded by an Episcopal priest, Tilden Edwards. Phone: 301-897-7334.

4) Retreats International (Notre Dame, IN)—a Catholic clearinghouse of retreat information that offers programs and publications, including a directory listing hundreds of retreat centers. Phone: 574-247-4443.

For a useful listing of many other centers for prayer and meditation, you may wish to consult *Sanctuaries: A Guide to Lodgings in Monasteries, Abbeys, and Retreats*, written by Jack and Marcia Kelly. Most of the places described are "contemplative communities which invite people to share their life and prayer," and generally they welcome people of all faiths, though they themselves grow out of particular traditions. Christian, Buddhist, Hindu, Sufi, and Jewish communities are represented. There are three books in this superb series, all published by Bell Tower in New York: *The Complete United States, The Northeast,* and *The West Coast and Southwest.*

Further Reading

The following list includes mostly books currently in print at the time of this writing—for the purpose of providing suggestions that will be most easily accessible to the reader, and also to keep the list within bounds. For this second edition, I have included two more recent works in the section describing Christian books on prayer; but otherwise, these are all works whose publication precedes the first edition printing in 1998.

Books of Mother Teresa's Spiritual Wisdom
These works can be divided into two categories: relatively small "gems" (volumes aimed at offering a good but limited sampling of thoughts) and books striving to be more definitive. All are explicitly Christ-centered (some more centrally than others), and all treat Mother Teresa's thoughts on prayer as one of at

least a few themes. Primarily biographical works are beyond the scope of this bibliography.

Slimmer Books

In the Heart of the World: Thoughts, Prayers, and Stories (New World Library, Novato, CA, 1997). A fine edition of luminous selections edited by Becky Benenate.

Meditations from A Simple Path (Ballantine Books, NY, 1996). Excerpts from the larger book, *A Simple Path* (see below), composed entirely of Mother Teresa's own words and spiritual teaching. Another lovingly produced gift edition brimming with Mother Teresa's timeless pearls of wisdom.

In My Own Words (Gramercy Books, NY, 1996). Pearls arranged according to fifteen themes. Edited by Jose Luis Gonzalez-Balado, one of the long-standing editors of Mother Teresa's written works.

Words to Love By, compiled by Frank J. Cunningham (Ave Maria Press, Notre Dame, IN, 1983). Poetically presented text highlighting the glories and challenges of Mother Teresa's message, with frequent photos.

The Best Gift is Love: Meditations by Mother Teresa (Servant Publications, Ann Arbor, MI, 1982). Like *Words to Love By* in its basic approach—highlights of Mother Teresa's instructions and reflections, poetically presented on the page, with many photos interspersed. Compiled by Sean-Patrick Lovett.

Blessings of Love (Servant Publications, Ann Arbor, MI, 1996). A sweet collection of brief inspirational sayings gathered from several of the other Servant Publication works listed below. Edited by Nancy Sabbag.

A Gift for God: Prayers and Meditations (Harper San Francisco, San Francisco, CA, U.S. edition, 1975). One of the earliest short collections of reflections, and a kind of companion work to Malcolm Muggeridge's classic 1971 biographical sketch *Something Beautiful for God*.

Larger Works
No Greater Love (New World Library, Novato, CA, 1997). A wonderfully comprehensive and accessible collection organized in eleven themes, followed by a conversation with Mother Teresa and a biographical sketch. Edited by Becky Benenate and Joseph Durepos; foreword by Thomas Moore. Also now available in the U.S. in a Spanish edition (*El Amor Mas Grande*).

A Simple Path (Ballantine Books, NY, 1995). A perfect introduction to Mother Teresa's work and teachings, this book contains not only Mother Teresa's spiritual principles but also the experiences of them by other memebers of her Order and volunteers. Compiled and introduced by Lucinda Vardey. Contains an appendix with important dates in Mother Teresa's life and another with information on the Order she founded, the Missionaries of Charity.

My Life for the Poor (Harper and Row, New York, NY, 1985), edited by Jose Luis Gonzalez-Balado and Janet N. Playfoot. A series of autobiographical stories, outlining the arc of Mother Teresa's life, with many jewels of her central teachings embedded within it.

The Joy in Loving: A Guide to Daily Living with Mother Teresa (Viking Penguin, NY, original copyright in India 1996). Reflections, one for each day of the year, covering a wide range of topics. Two long-time associates of Mother Teresa's, Jaya Chaliha and Father Edward Le Joly, compiled this stirring collection. Father Le Joly, who was Mother Teresa's spiritual advisor and the author of a major biography of Mother Teresa, also provides a detailed introduction to the history of her work. The thoughts are presented as short sayings in stanza form. While not organized by theme, contains a useful thematic index. These editors published *Reaching Out in Love: Stories Told by Mother Teresa* in 2000 (Continuum), also strongly recommended.

Love: A Fruit Always in Season (Ignatius Press, San Francisco, CA, 1987). A far-ranging book of daily meditations, arranged according to the Catholic calendar and also by theme. An excellent selection edited by Dorothy S. Hunt, drawing upon many earlier works, all of which are cited—a real help for knowing where the meditations first appeared.

Total Surrender (Servant Publications, Ann Arbor, MI, 1985). A rich spiritual sourcebook of excerpts from the constitution of Mother Teresa's Order as well as her instructions and letters within the Order. Comprehensive. Edited by Brother Angelo Devananda.

Jesus: The Word to be Spoken: Meditations for Every Day of the Year (Servant Publications, Ann Arbor, MI, 1986). Another well-done collection by Brother Angelo Devananda, this one arranged in calendar form.

One Heart Full of Love (Servant Publications, Ann Arbor, MI, original copyright in Spain 1984). A variety of rousing talks, interviews, and correspondence, with an emphasis on loving the poor and the blessings of sharing. Edited by Jose Luis Gonzalez-Balado.

Loving Jesus (Servant Publications, Ann Arbor, MI, 1991). Another collection of dynamic addresses edited by Jose Luis Gonzalez-Balado, including a long interview and a biographical sketch.

Heart of Joy: The Transforming Power of Self-Giving (Servant Publications, Ann Arbor, MI, 1987). Yet another worthwhile Gonzalez-Balado compendium of Mother Teresa's words, gathered from a variety of sources.

Prayertimes with Mother Teresa: A New Adventure in Prayer Involving Scripture, Mother Teresa, and You (Image Books, New York, NY, 1989). For each week of the year, a passage from the Bible, a story by or about Mother Teresa, and a spiritual reflection from her. Edited by Eileen and Kathleen Egan. The main text is followed by a "seven-day retreat" section with suggested prayers, litanies, and meditations.

Works of Love Are Works of Peace: Mother Teresa of Calcutta and the Missionaries of Charity (Ignatius Press, San Francisco, 1996). One of the stunning books of photos available, this one has selections of Mother Teresa's counsel, including a letter on prayer, as well as a full collection of the Order's prayers.

Among other closely related books of interest, perhaps most notable is *Suffering into Joy* by Eileen and Kathleen Egan, (Servant Publications), which contains passages from Mother Teresa's teachings. See above for publisher's information.

Further Books on Prayer
There are many good books on prayer. The list below is far from exhaustive but includes some of this editor's favorite ones. They are restricted to books entirely about prayer, rather than ones that may contain a chapter or two on the subject. The emphasis is on practical, down-to-earth guides that are most likely to further the actual practice of prayer. Books of prayers are not included.

Books Addressed Equally to Christians and Non-Christians
Larry Dossey, *Prayer Is Good Medicine* (Harper San Francisco, San Francisco, CA, 1996). The author, who wrote the Foreword to *Everything Starts from Prayer* and is a highly regarded physician and thinker, describes this book as "a heart-to-heart talk."

Dossey wisely discusses prayer and common misconceptions about prayer, with a special focus on the relations between prayer, healing, and science. The longest of four sections is called "How to Pray." (See also Dossey's more detailed, scholarly *Healing Words: The Power of Prayer and the Practice of Medicine* and his more recent thoughtful book *Be Careful What You Pray For*.)

James P. Carse, *The Silence of God: Meditations on Prayer* (Harper San Francisco, San Francisco, CA, 1985). An NYU professor of religion brings simplicity together with philosophic depth to his writings on prayer. Four graceful, grounded meditations about speaking to God. Incisive yet subtly heart-centered.

Richard Chilson, *You Shall Not Want: A Spiritual Journey Based on the Psalms* (Ave Maria Press, Notre Dame, IN, 1996). A guide to prayer using brief selections and phrases from the psalms arranged for the thirty days in a month. Gently presented. From Ave Maria's "30 Days with a great Spiritual Teacher" Series, whose other volumes are also recommended.

Matthew Fox, *On Becoming a Musical Mystical Bear: Spirituality American Style* (Paulist Press, New York, NY, 1972). Simultaneously whimsical and serious, Fox takes a contemplative activist's look at "what prayer is" and "what prayer isn't." He presents his ideas of "creation spirituality" in the process, and whereas he doesn't present prayer here in the precise "how to" terms of a spiritual practice, he underscores points that many people inclined to withdraw from the world in the name of "dedicated spiritual practice" all too easily overlook.

Dale Salwak (editor) *The Power of Prayer* (New World Library, Novato, CA, 1999). A multifaith anthology that includes contributions by Mother Teresa and this editor. (Currently out of print but worthwhile finding used on the Internet.) Also see *The Flowering of the Soul: A Book of Prayers by Women* (Lucinda Vardey, editor), which offers an approach to praying through experiences and counsel of women from diverse traditions, including Mother Teresa.

Christian Books on Prayer

If you don't feel entirely comfortable calling yourself "Christian," yet you begin to read Christian writings, here's a suggestion: consider a different name that works for you. If the term "Christian" doesn't feel like a full fit, when you come across it on the page, substitute "a truly good person," "an open and growing person," "a holy person," "a person trying her or his very best," "a student of prayer," or "a sincere spiritual seeker." Where devotion to Jesus is discussed, this may not quite hit the mark, but where universal insights about devotion, prayer, and inner work are the subjects, it will. There may be legitimate objections to this idea. Nonetheless, it seems that "Christian" or other designations like "Jew" or "Muslim" are often used within their own groups as synonyms for "a truly good person." When used as such, they are a residue of a more provincial era. Let's try at times to open ourselves to writings of our brothers and sisters in other cultures, and to translate basic insights across these differing traditions, for the sake of discovering our common humanity, our common soul.

Henri J.M. Nouwen, *The One Necessary Thing: Living a Prayerful Life* (Crossroad, NY, original copyright 1999). This book is similar to the present collection, in that it is a labor of love compiled by my late friend Wendy Wilson Greer, bringing together Nouwen's thoughts on prayer from his diverse range of books. Greer was a good friend of Nouwen's, and Nouwen, a Catholic priest who died in 1996, is rightly cherished as one of the finest modern writers about the spiritual journey.

Metropolitan Anthony (Anthony Bloom), Volume in *The Modern Spirituality Series* (Templegate, Springfield, IL, 1987). The most concise introduction to a first-rate contemporary writer on prayer. The author was a former medical doctor and French resistance fighter turned Russian Orthodox priest and church leader who died in 2003. ("Metropolitan" is something like "Cardinal" in the Eastern Orthodox church.) The book is an offering of page-long selections from earlier works, and it contains a convenient reference to all of these works at the end, among which *Beginning to Pray* and *Living Prayer* are especially recommended.

Douglas V. Steere, *Dimensions of Prayer* (Upper Room Books, Nashville, TN, original copyright 1962). A succinct and down-to-earth classic on prayer by a scholar and Quaker leader. Steere, a philosophy professor at Haverford, was the main Quaker representative at Vatican II and an early pioneer of ecumenical dialogue with Buddhists and Hindus. A document he wrote for Quaker organizational purposes eventually became the blueprint for the Peace Corps. He shares with Metropolitan Anthony a great gift for the telling vignette.

Thomas Keating, *Open Mind, Open Heart: The Contemplative Dimension of the Gospel* (Element Books, Rockport, ME, 1994). In 1975, a few Catholic monks came together and crafted a method called "centering prayer." Father Keating provides one of the clearest step-by-step descriptions of this approach, which simplifies age-old spiritual wisdom meaningfully for our time. Among its best points, Keating offers sound advice regarding "distracting thoughts" and inner obstacles to praying in general. It should be emphasized that the approach outlined is a high form of practice that isn't meant to exclude other forms. See also M. Basil Pennington's *Centering Prayer* and William A. Meninger's *The Loving Search for God*.

Philip Yancey, *Prayer: Does It Make Any Difference?* (Zondervan, Grand Rapids, MI, 2006). This is the most recent book in the bibliography. Yancey never disappoints. Like Richard Foster, whose own superb book on prayer is listed below, Yancey is highly intelligent and articulate, and he has thought seriously as a Christian about matters of the spirit for a long time. His honest vulnerability is perhaps his greatest gift to us. The "Prayer Resources" at the book's end offers Yancey's own annotated listing of Christian books about prayer and is more up-to-date than my own.

Ken Gire (editor), *Between Heaven and Earth: Prayers and Reflections That Celebrate An Intimate God* (Harper San Francisco, San Francisco, CA, 1997). An unusually good collection of reflections about prayer interspersed with some prayers themselves. Passages are mainly from well-known writers like

C.S. Lewis, Richard Foster, Abraham Joshua Heschel, Larry Dossey, Dietrich Bonhoeffer, and many others you may well recognize. Various faith traditions are included, though the sources are primarily Christian.

Among the numerous other noteworthy Christian books about prayer as spiritual practice, please keep in mind the following titles: Brother David Steindl-Rast, *Gratefulness, The Hearth of Prayer: An Approach to Life in Fullness*; Richard J. Foster, *Prayer: Finding the Heart's True Home*; Tilden Edwards, *Living in Presence: Spiritual Exercises to Open Your Life to the Awareness of God*; Martin Helldorfer, *Prayer When It's Hard to Pray*; Thomas Kelly, *A Testament of Devotion*; Richard J. Foster and James Bryan Smith, *Devotional Classics*; Thomas Merton, *Contemplative Prayer* (the introduction by Zen master Thich Naht Hanh and foreword by Douglas Steere are treats in themselves); Gabriel Galache, *Praying Body and Soul: Methods and Practices of Anthony De Mello*; John R. Yungblut, *Rediscovering Prayer*; and Patricia Loring, *Listening Spirituality* (available from the Pendle Hill online store).

Jewish Books on Prayer

The note about the word "Christian" above applies equally to the word "Jew." Even as we honor our own traditions, we need to remember that historically a wounded antagonism has separated groups of believers and has colored their views of other groups. We need not only to remember, but also to forget: to do our utmost to acknowledge it in ourselves, work with it, and slowly (or immediately!) get beyond it. Let's not, in any case, deprive ourselves of the inspiration and insight contained in other sacred traditions, even in works purportedly aimed only at a single group of believers.

Arthur Green and Barry W. Holtz (editors and translators), *Your Word Is Fire: The Hasidic Masters on Contemplative Prayer* (Jewish Lights Publishing, Woodstock, VT, 1977). Parables and sayings from the extraordinary Hasidic literature on prayer, presented in verse form, with a brief introduction that serves admirably as a summary of Hasidic thought. Edited by two leaders of the Jewish renewal movement.

Yitzhak Buxbaum, *Real Davvening: Jewish Prayer as a Form of Meditation for Beginning and Experienced Davveners* (Jewish Spirit, New York, 1996). "Davvening" is a Jewish word for praying. This booklet explicitly aims to provide the reader hints for meeting God in prayer. In other words, it offers an explanation of the spiritual side of Jewish worship and contains simple traditional techniques for how to experience God's presence during communal devotional services. Readily applicable to other traditions. See also Buxbaum's much more detailed work, *Jewish Spiritual Practices*, especially chapters five and six. Google "Jewish Spirit" to buy these works online. Buxbaum is a dedicated teacher as well as a good friend of the editor's.

Rabbi Nachman, *Tsohar* ("Light") (Breslov Research Institute, New York, NY, 1986). The 18th and 19th century Hasidic tradition is a wonderful source of practical wisdom about prayer, and Rabbi Nachman of Breslov (or "Bratslav") was one of its greatest teachers. This booklet, which centers on the power of "just one true word" in prayer, is one of several valuable booklets published by The Breslov Research Institute. Other recommended ones include *Outpouring of the Soul* and *Restore My Soul.*

Sidney Greenburg, *A Treasury of Thoughts on Jewish Prayer* (Jason Aronson, Northvale, NJ, 1989). A rich anthology of short selections from many sources, including the Talmud, the Hasidic masters, and contemporary thinkers. These are intelligently selected and heartfelt passages with a scope wider than the question "how to pray"—but consistently good food for thought and inspiration for worship.

Islamic Books on Prayer

Prayer is central to Islamic spirituality. One of the five "pillars" of Islam is daily prayer (*salat*), which consists of a series of movements enacted while reciting suras, or chapters, from the Qur'an. Other forms of prayer include *du'a*, or personal entreaties and petitions; *dhikr*, or meditative remembrance on a sacred word or phrase; and *munajat*, or devotional conversations between lover and the divine beloved. A helpful introduction and sourcebook to prayer in Islam: Constance Padwick, *Muslim Devotions: A Study of Prayer Manuals in Common Use* (Oneworld Publications, Oxford, England, 1996; original copyright 1961).

Sources & Acknowledgements

Wholehearted appreciation is due Sister Priscilla and the Missionaries of Charity in Calcutta for granting permission for the compilation of this collection and for their input in the process. A portion of the receipts from the sale of this book will go to the Missionaries of Charity. For more information on the work of the Order, search online or contact one of its U.S. houses: 335 E. 145th St., Bronx, NY 10451 and 1596 Fulton St., San Francisco, CA 94117.

I have tried to leave no stone unturned in my efforts to obtain permissions. If there are oversights I would request that the aggrieved party contact me so that I may get it right for the third edition.

It should be mentioned that there is a considerable overlap in Mother Teresa's writings. I have cited one source for each passage in this volume, but many of these meditations can be found in a few different books.

Where sources have been printed in hardcover and paperback editions, the page numbers below refer to the hardcover edition.

Grateful acknowledgements to:

New World Library for permission to reprint from the following seven works: *No Greater Love* (called simply "Love" below) (New World Library, New York, NY, 1997), edited by Becky Benenate and Joseph Durepos; *Total Surrender* (called simply "Surrender" below) (Servant Books, Ann Arbor, MI, 1985), edited by Brother Angelo Devananda; *Jesus, the Word to Be Spoken: Prayers and Meditations for Every Day of the Year* (called simply "Jesus" below) (Servant Books, Ann Arbor, MI, 1986), compiled by Brother Angelo Devananda; *Heart of Joy* (called simply "Heart" below) (Servant Books, Ann Arbor, MI, 1987), edited by Jose Luis Gonzalez-Balado; *One Heart Full of Love* (called simply "Full" below) (Servant Books, Ann Arbor, MI, 1984), edited by Jose Luis Gonzalez-Balado; *Loving Jesus* (called simply "Loving" below) (Servant Books, Ann Arbor, MI, 1991), edited by Jose Luis Gonzalez-Balado; *Suffering into Joy* (called simply "Suffering" below) (Servant Books, Ann Arbor, MI, 1996), written by Eileen and Kathleen Egan;

to Penguin India for permission to reprint from *The Joy in Loving* (called simply "Joy" below) (Viking Penguin, New York, NY, original copyright 1996), compiled by Jaya Chaliha and Edward Le Joly;

to Ballantine Books for permission to reprint from *A Simple Path* (called simply "Path" below) (Ballantine, New York, NY, 1995), compiled by Lucinda Vardey;

to SPCK (the Society to Promote Christian Knowledge) for permission to reprint from the following two works: *Life in the Spirit* (simply called "Spirit" below) (Harper and Row, San Francisco, CA, 1983), edited by Kathryn Spink; *I Need Souls Like You* (called simply "Souls" below) (Harper and Row, San Francisco, CA, 1984), edited by Kathryn Spink;

to HarperCollins and HarperCollins United Kingdom for permission to reprint from the following five works: *My Life for the Poor* (called simply "Life" below) (Harper and Row, New York, NY, 1985), edited by Jose Luis Gonzalez-Balado and Janet N. Playfoot; *The Love of Christ: Spiritual Counsels, Mother Teresa of Calcutta* (called simply "Christ" below) (Harper and Row, San Francisco, CA, 1982), edited by Georges Corree and Jean Barbier; *A Gift for God: Mother Teresa of Calcutta* (called simply "Gift" below) (Harper and Row, New York, NY, 1975); *Mother Teresa: Her People and Her Work* (called simply "People" below) (Harper and Row, New York, NY, 1976), edited by Desmond Doig; *Mother Teresa of Calcutta: A Biography* (called simply "Calcutta" below) (Harper and Row, San Francisco, CA, 1983), by Edward Le Joly;

to Liguori Publications and Jose Luis Gonzalez-Balado for permission to reprint from the following two works: *In My Own Words* (called simply "Words" below) (Liguori, Liguori, MO, 1996), compiled by Jose Luis Gonzalez-Balado (page numbers in the new Gramercy Books edition are noted with "GB" preceding); *Always the Poor* (called simply "Always" below) (Liguori, MO, 1980), edited by Jose Luis Gonzalez-Balado;

to Ave Maria Press for permission to reprint from *Words to Love By* (called simply "Words" below) (Ave Maria Press, Notre Dame, IN, 1983), compiled by Frank J. Cunningham.

Other Sources

Love: A Fruit Always in Season, edited by Dorothy Hunt, (called simply "Fruit" below) (Ignatius Press, San Francisco, CA, 1987).

Works of Love Are Works of Peace: Mother Teresa of Calcutta and the Missionaries of Charity, edited with photographs by Michael Collopy (called simply "Works" below) (Ignatius Press, San Francisco, CA, 1996).

Mother Teresa by Navin Chawla (called simply "Mother" below) (Element Books, Rockport, ME, 1992).

Such a Vision of the Street by Eileen Egan (called simply "Vision" below) (Doubleday, New York, NY, 1985).

Sources of Specific Passages:

p. 1: *Joy*, p. 43

p. 2, top passage: *Jesus*, p. 21

p. 2, bottom passage: *Spirit*, p. 82

p. 3: *Surrender*, p. 109

p. 4, top passage: *Heart*, p. 98

p. 4, bottom passage: *Jesus*, p. 74

p. 5, top passage: *Joy*, p. 325

p. 5, bottom passage: *Path*, p. 19

p. 6: *Spirit*, pp. 38-39

p. 7, top passage: *Christ*, p. 48

p. 7, bottom passage: *Spirit*, p. 65

p. 8: *Calcutta*, pp. 227-28

p. 9, top passage: *Spirit*, p. 72

p. 9, bottom passage: *Heart*, p. 123

p. 10: *Joy*, p. 96

p. 11: *Spirit*, p. 82

p. 12, top passage: *Joy*, p. 159

p. 12, bottom passage: *Joy*, p. 260

p. 13: *Words*, p. 103 (GB: p. 51)

p. 14, top passage: *Words*, p. 104 (GB: p. 51)

p. 14, bottom passage: *Surrender*, p. 98

p. 15: *Words*, p. 36 (GB: p. 11)

p. 19, top passage: *Christ*, p. 8

p. 19, bottom passage: *Life*, p. 100

p. 20: *Christ*, p. 8

p. 21, top passage: *Life*, p. 101

p. 21, bottom passage: *Joy*, p. 114

p. 22, top passage: *Joy*, p. 127

p. 22, bottom passage: *Surrender*, p. 106

p. 23, top and bottom passages: *Love*, pp. 9-10

p. 74: *Love*, p. 5
p. 75, top passage: *Love*, p. 4
p. 75, bottom passage: *Christ*, p. 84
p. 76, top passage: *Love*, p. 14
p. 76, bottom passage: *Jesus*, p. 7
p. 76: *Spirit*, p. 35
p. 78, top passage: *Spirit*, p. 37
p. 78, bottom passage: *Christ*, p. 112
p. 79: *Fruit*, p. 214
p. 80, top passage: *Spirit*, pp. 68-69
p. 80, bottom passage: *Love*, p. 112
p. 81, top passage: *Christ*, p. 9
p. 81, bottom passage: *Spirit*, p. 24
p. 82, top passage: *Joy*, p. 115
p. 82, bottom passage: *People*, pp. 145-46
p. 83: *Path*, p. 14
p. 84: *Path*, p. 14
p. 85, top passage: *Path*, p. 14
p. 85, bottom passage: *Path*, p. 14
p. 86: *Path*, p. 20
p. 87: *Path*, pp. 14-15
p. 88, top passage: *Joy*, p. 107
p. 88, bottom passage: *Fruit*, p. 110
p. 89, top passage: *Spirit*, p. 35
p. 89, bottom passage: *Spirit*, p. 35
p. 90, top passage: *Joy*, p. 136
p. 90, bottom passage: *Christ*, p. 103
p. 91, top passage: *Spirit*, p. 68
p. 91, bottom passage: *Jesus*, p. 121
p. 92 (All but the first line, which recurs throughout Mother Teresa's writings.): *Joy*, p. 103 (in this passage, Mother Teresa has drawn from Isaiah 43:1-4 and 49:15-16)

p. 93, top passage: *Joy*, p. 127

p. 93, bottom passage: *Love*, p. 4

p. 94: *Love*, p. 6 (Compare St. Augustine's beautiful words: "My whole heart I lay upon the altar of thy praise, a holocaust of praise I offer to Thee. Let the flame of Thy love set on fire my whole heart; may I wholly burn toward Thee, wholly on fire toward Thee, wholly Thee as though set aflame by Thee." Quoted in Douglas V. Steere, *Beginning from Within*, p. 110.)

p. 99, top passage: *Surrender*, p. 103

p. 99, bottom passage: *Joy*, p. 273

p. 100, top passage: *Life*, p. 100

p. 100, bottom passage: *Love*, p. 7

p. 101: *Surrender*, p. 106

p. 102: *Surrender*, p. 111

p. 103, top passage: *Christ*, p. 9

p. 103, bottom passage: *Surrender*, p. 108 (The last sentence is from Psalm 46:10.)

p. 107, top passage: *Surrender*, p. 107

p. 107, middle passage: *Life*, p. 101 (A lovely way of putting what the psalmist, Meister Eckhart, St. Augustine, St. Thomas Aquinas, and many others have said. Any claim of originality would have been antithetical to Mother Teresa.)

p. 107, bottom passage: *Spirit*, p. 45

p. 108, top passage: *Words*, p. 160

p. 108, middle passage: *Christ*, p. 52

p. 108, bottom passage: *Spirit*, p. 45

p. 109, top passage: *Words*, p. 44

p. 109, bottom passage: *Heart*, p. 82

p. 110, top passage: *Path*, p. 7

p. 110, bottom passage: *Surrender*, pp. 111-112

p. 111, top passage: *Jesus*, p. 59

p. 135, top passage: *Spirit*, pp. 24-25
p. 135, bottom passage: *Joy*, p. 187
p. 136: *Joy*, p. 141
p. 137: *Spirit*, p. 81
p. 138, top and bottom passages: *Surrender*, p. 114
p. 139: *Spirit*, p. 45
p. 140: *Spirit*, p. 49
p. 141: *Life*, p. 41
p. 142, top and bottom passages: *Spirit*, p. 7
p. 143, top passage: *Surrender*, p. 99
p. 143, bottom passage: *Joy*, p. 114
p. 144: *Joy*, p. 171

Further Acknowledgements
First let me simply offer sincere thanks for all the friends who helped. You know who you are.

Heartfelt gratitude to my original publisher Steven Scholl and the three literary agents involved at various stages—Kim Witherspoon, Gideon Weil, and Michele Rubin. I've also greatly appreciated the White Cloud Press team who has taken over where Steven left off: Stephen Sendar, Gary Kliewer, Christy Collins, and Raina Hassan. Their enthusiasm for this book has been a joy.

Many thanks are due all of my family, and especially my wife, Laura, and our three children Charles, Joe, and Marguerite, for bearing with the time this work has required of me.

A particular group in the publishing world did work absolutely crucial to my own—the editors and publishers of earlier compilations of Mother Teresa's wisdom, including Dorothy Hunt, Lucinda Vardey, Becky Benenate, Father Edward Le Joly, Bert Ghezzi, Jose Luis Gonzalez-Balado, Kathryn Spink, Brother Angelo Devananda, Eileen Egan, Kathleen Egan, Joseph Durepos, Desmond Doig, and Jaya Chaliha. The first five in this group gave generously of their time to me directly, providing further assistance to make this book possible. Others in the publishing world who supported the project included Peter Edelman, Kris Kleimann, Amy Edelman, Paul Cash, and Marcia Broucek. Marcia also reminded me of the important gender issues involved with Mother Teresa's language.

Grateful thanks to Janet Murphy and all the staff at the Hastings-on-Hudson Public Library, for their endless interlibrary loan efforts. Rowie Edelman and Debbie Boylan at the now defunct Good Yarns Bookstore also gave valuable assistance.

Thanks also to Sarah Sprague, Aaron Silverman, and Molly Maguire for their support of this book.

Finally, I'd like to express my deep gratitude to three people who are now all deceased. In my own pre-teen and teen years, they introduced me to the world of prayer: Annie Lee, Frank J. Bertino, and Rudi.